# *Grateful & Hateful*

A Collection of Poems
Rose Quinn

Copyright © 2025 Rose Quinn.

All rights reserved. This book or any portion thereof may not be reproduced or used in any manner whatsoever without the express written permission of the author except for the use of brief quotations in a book review.

IBSN: [979-8-218-59407-7]

Cover: Artwork by Lucy Quinn

Author's Biography: Joanie Quinn, Worlds Best Mom

Illustrations: Rose Quinn

**Table of Contents:**

*Foreword*..................................................................7
- *Lovely Bones*..................................................9

*Summer*.................................................................11
- *Beautiful Day in the Neighborhood*..........12
- *Sylvia's Tree*..................................................14
- *Phoenix*..........................................................15
- *my girls*..........................................................16
- *My Dear Whimsy*..........................................18
- *Peter Pan Plan*..............................................19
- *Systemic infection*........................................20
- *Family Dinners*.............................................21
- *Pick up the Pace*..........................................22
- *The Ditch*......................................................23
- *Tonic and Gin*...............................................24
- *Marilyn and Me*............................................25
- *Social Garden*...............................................26
- *symbiotic or competitive?*..........................27
- *Forgiving Tree*...............................................28
- *Stuck*...............................................................29

*Fire Season*..........................................................31
- *Ode to Nana*..................................................32
- *Quarter Test*..................................................33
- *Withering Petals*...........................................34
- *Samson's Speed*............................................35
- *Haunted*.........................................................36
- *Sisters*............................................................37
- *Before the Apple was Torn*.........................38
- *Where to Go*..................................................39
- *Nylons*............................................................40
- *Tired*...............................................................41
- *Attempt to Cheer*..........................................42
- *Deck of Cards*................................................43

- Past Selves............44
- alone with me ............45
- forgotten spines............46
- Wrap It Up............47

**Winter**............**49**
- Separate and Shared............49
- A rose is a rose is a rose............50
- Trepidation Station............51
- how to get back............52
- Delicate Scarring............53
- Grateful and Hateful............54
- the bin............55
- Caught............56
- how to spot a foe............57
- Muffled............58
- the pitcher............59
- Borrowed or Blue?............60
- the mirror............61
- Recipe for Nostalgia............62
- Brief Grief............63
- Currency............64
- Cliché............65

**Spring**............**67**
- Truth............68
- Hunger............69
- Pretty in Pink............70
- my cherry tree............71
- is this a safe subject?............72
- A Brain Like Me............73
- Occupied............74
- So it Goes............75
- Perfection Perception............76
- All Me ............77

- *Purgatory...............................................78*
- *a warning................................................79*
- *In Wait....................................................80*
- *Jumping In..............................................81*
- *Who.........................................................82*
- *Finally Me...............................................83*
- *Scenery....................................................84*

***Acknowledgements..............................................85***

This book is dedicated to my family.
Thank you for being my safety

"I've heard people say proudly that they have no original thoughts- Wouldn't that be nice? I have so many original thoughts I have to take medication for it."-Mark Vonnegut

## Foreword

I write the foreword to this vulnerable and terrifying collection of poems on my mother's 63rd birthday. Her mother, and the mothers before her run through my veins in a way that language could never convey. The determination, endurance, and adaptability of the women throughout my family allows me to have the voice I have today.

I wrote these poems over the last 6 years as I graduated college, lost my grandfather and grandmother, moved to live on my own, laughed and cried with my family, and lost more people I thought would be in my life forever. I hold space in my heart for every person I've crossed paths with, and I wish I could share every poem I wrote about them.

This past half-decade, I have grown into someone I would not have recognized at 16. I've heard poems take shape in my head throughout these moments, and I can't keep them to myself anymore. I can only wish that my writing may influence someone in a way that all the writers I hold dear to my heart have shaped me.

I owe everything to my family. My parents embody love and care in a way I will forever be grateful for. My siblings teasing and encouragement lives in every fiber of my being, and I will never have the words to thank them for growing up with me. My Nana and Papa, who displayed my first poems in frames on their walls, have never felt closer to me than when I began to put this collection together. I see their lightness in every sunset.

All that to say; this collection is a story of full of love and loss and love again. I somehow lost myself among this, and have been slowly climbing my way back towards a future I can't wait to live in. The girl in me who discovered poetry would be in awe of the way I've surrendered to it today. I'm so proud to make her happy.

Without further ado:

*Lovely Bones*

My bones, they're hollow
yours must be too
Lacking their marrow
mirrored solitude
There's always tomorrow
a sentiment untrue
I'll plead to borrow
Some marrow from you

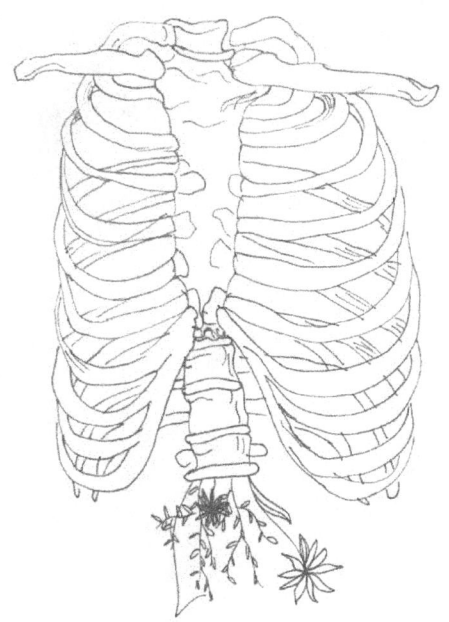

# *Summer*

Whatever I become
this becomes me
The air and the trees
breathing with me

*Beautiful Day in the Neighborhood*

Dancing swifts pepper cobalt sky
they seem to float more than fly
At once they're off in another direction
together as one with effortless connection

The music in my ear pauses
as my pocket buzzes
I say hello to my mother
she asks if I'm sitting with another

My eyes explore the grass ahead of me
as I chuckle at the beautiful irony
when I answer simply, "no"
Yet even so-

Two men near me give off the energy of dads
watching the birds move like they're recording the stats
Arms crossed over their chests like twins-
I find myself using my hand to cover my grin

The couple in front of me sits with each other
leaning on and somehow supporting one another
The scraping of skateboards on pavement in the park
sends the scattered dogs into unified barks

The younger kids are yawning wide-
as the birds twirl to the side
The only place where no one seems to be in a hurry
the distinction of them above and us below becomes blurry

Once I've said goodbye to my mother
my attention returns to the swifts as they hover
in the darkening lilac sky, but they whip around
suddenly darting like a quiver of arrows down-

Dashing into the brick chimney of the elementary school
but just when they have us fooled
One leads the others to linger awhile longer
anticipation amongst the crowd grows stronger

At last, each and every wing gives in to the need for rest-
the neighbors below look to each other to test
Whether the final swift has finally found home because
once the sky is truly empty the grass erupts in applause

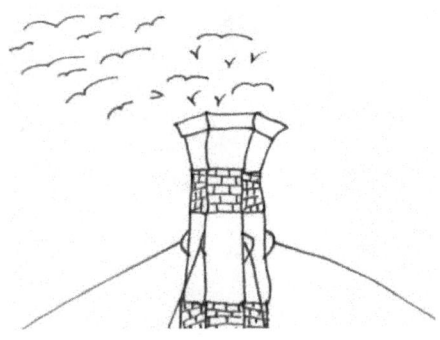

*Sylvia's Tree*

I am afraid
all of my words will go unread
all of my thoughts will remain unsaid
and I will shrivel like Sylvia's fig tree
never revealing I loved the way you
cared for me

*Phoenix*

I run I hide I jump
I tip I tilt I bump
I land I break I sunk
I'm cracking into chunks
I choke I spit I swallow
Suddenly I'm hollow
I float I drift I wallow
I wish away my sorrow
I swim I push I climb
I'll leave myself behind
I lift I pull I spring
I swallow the lightning
I run I hide I jump

I forget about the bumps

*my girls*

My girls, you see
they're everything to me
We clutch one another
over hilarity we discover

We dance and sing audibly
not well, but not terribly
Wiping each others tears
confiding in our various fears

We read and we run
pretending both are fun
Savoring each others insights
disecting dramatic Bravo fights

We paint and we create
we let our grievances permeate
gifted art we place upon the walls
Staring at them over long distance calls

Bright flashes in photo booths
capturing our joyous youth
Shoving annoying men away
grudgingly letting gentlemen stay

I'll watch her grieve him
witness the evolution of her whims
watch the beauty return to her sins
We're better off without them

I suppose I could give you away
if they promised they would always
& forever take care of you the same way
all us girls would anyway.

*My Dear Whimsy*

I've been searching for quite a while
to discover the source of running water,
the end of the rainbow so to speak
turning to my dear Whimsy when life gets bleak
colors swirling in waterfall's floating mist
stars hitting my skin basking in her bliss
she dances with me in the frigid river
hips shifting against currents' shivers
letting the sun plant her lips on my skin
blooming freckles in the likes of my kin
Whimsy and me, we have a way of meeting
in the most uncertain of scenery
she's shown up in the rain and the gloom
stood by me admiring withering tombs
gently turning me to take in the view
our mountains shining in their familiar queue

If age takes anything from me.
Let it not be my dear, Whimsy.

*Peter Pan Plan*

There is a blond woman
in my peripheral vision
flashing as I pass alleys and intersections

I'm dancing next to a mirror
she seems to love the idea
her blond braid swings
just as mine twirls
her freckles round as pearls

Someday I'll have to come to terms
that she is me and I am her
blooming aging lines
I refuse to claim as mine
Peter Pan reincarnated
Do you think I'll ever blame it?

*systemic infection*

Relief fills my head as I put down the book I just read
my brother and sister sit on adjacent hotel beds
knowing we'll be home before the next sunset
meant I thought we were past getting upset

Too soon my sister's eyes were on fire
I watch as my brother's walls climb higher
the expanse between the beds
widening and cracking in my head

Laughter tossing a grenade across the abyss
pointed arrows returned in defense with a hiss
wishing to become one with the shadow at my feet
I beg just one of them to admit defeat

Whenever there's a crack in our connection
I fear it will become a systemic infection
I'd cease to have a shadow for too long without my kin
how can anyone understand the place that puts us in?

*Family Dinners*

Sundays we have family dinners
where we laugh loud as sinners
Mom always has the table ready
Dad's down at the bar pouring steadily
Soon we'll sit and eat together
Throughout the seasons and weather
We clink and we snap, we jest and we pest
for just an hour we forget the rest
we pass the salad, discuss what's valid
we rotate around
who's living in town
but the table and chairs stay the same
and so does the strength in our name
after, Dad will take up at the sink
Mom and I will share and overthink
I'll glance at the clock
asking if anyone's got
a moment to spare
to take me away from here
my brother or my mother
my dad, someone or another
will sit behind the wheel
this is my favorite part of the deal
we'll take the long route for the appeal
at my home I'll begin to pout
but then I'll start to laugh about
the way Mom snorted
or how the dog farted
and know without a doubt
I wouldn't spend Sunday any other way
than at my parents house anyway

*Pick up the Pace*

I took a run by the river
I love to breathe hard with her
the air feels so much sweeter
when the fish and birds are nearer

I can run as fast and far as I want
desperately pushing to forget the taunts
All the things that feel like they haunt
my skin and bones whenever they want.

*The Ditch*

Can you hear the birds?
chirp, chirp, chirping
My pedals twist and click
unforgiving metal clutched in my grip
Chirp. Chirp. Chirp.
I recognize scenery again
just as my vision bends
      chirp. chirp. chirp.
The earth is soft and cold
metal and me together in fold
      chirp.chirp.chirp.
Tall figures pass the ditch I sit
I call but blood flies out with my spit
      chirp chirp chirp
Isn't that my mom and dad?
leaning over looking sad?
      chirp chirp chirp
No, it couldn't have been them
they wouldn't have left just then
     chirp
          chirp
              chirp
I won't be found
I'll sleep on the damp ground
Until the next time this dream comes back around.

*Tonic and Gin*

Me and him
We're tonic and gin
I'm bubbly, he's grim
It would be a waste
to miss out on the taste
together we make
quite the lovely take

*Marilyn and Me*

There's no space next to me
and I'm not making room.
You'd rather I defer to you
but you'll have to come for me in my tomb.
Like Marilyn's demise
you'll wish to be laid to rest just next to mine.
I'll warn you just once
it would take guts.
To plant yourself in the muck
anywhere within reach of my spiteful soul.
Next time they find you
your bones will resemble gritty coals.
My bones, they'll be pristine
built from bearing the weight of your bore.
My tomb will read
"Their regrets lie here."
Yours will say,
"Who cares?"

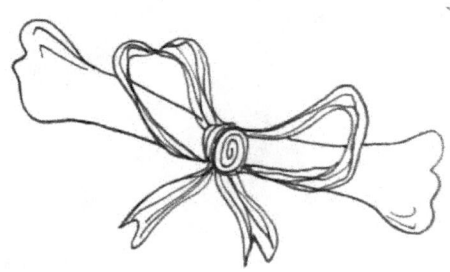

*Social Garden*

I cut, cut, cut,
prune, prune, prune,
sweat, sweat, sweet
air coming through to me
finally.

*symbiotic or competitive?*

that sky
she cries
the sea
it lies
I believed before,
now I know much more.

that sky
she supports
the sea
it snorts
at her contingency,
between you and me,

that sea
she hides
behind the skies
sealing the deal
on her choking appeal.

*Forgiving Tree*

Do you climb the same tree
in an attempt to feel close to me?
I close the same doors
I twist the same locks
I swear the doorknob talks
It whispers and snickers
watching me whither
Hiding in here,
in shame or in fear.

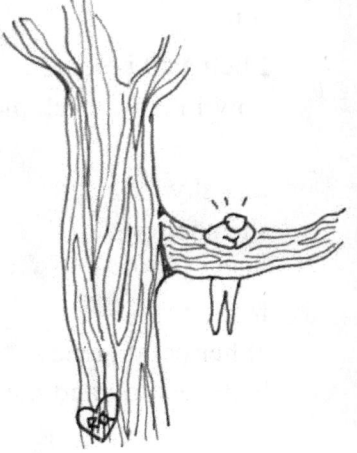

I can't be near that tree
it used to feel a part of me
I prefer her in memory
back when she was just mine
you hadn't yet claimed my time
partners in crime, she and I
Does she too regret letting you by?
My love for her carved in bark
she held my youth in her trunk
You never deserved her care
not that you were ever aware

I hope you think of me up there in the sap.
I hope I cross your mind as you hear the snap.

*Stuck*

the train horns blast
as the jet planes fly past
my feet are planted
rooted and cemented
longing to feel the rush of going that fast

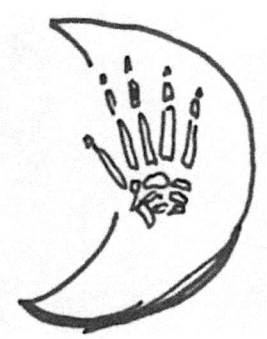

# *Fire Season*

I spend September reading on my fire escape. I hope I can remember come December.

*Ode to Nana*

"Young Lady You're Scaring Me"
has surprisingly come to be
a look I embody easily
thanks to my Nana's influencing

She's in the narrowing of my eyes
whenever a man brings up the lies
of how we're taught to be as young girls
the expression polished like a pearl

it involves bringing up a sneer
to instill fear in any man near
I've been told not to look at them like that
which only turns me into more of a brat

she is always in me
in how to stand and how to be
she'd be so proud of who I am
if she knew I was out here scaring men.

*Quarter Test*

Laundry day I pick out my quarters
carefully placing them in order
the familiar Eagle wings
are the first I bring
away from the other coins
ones they'll never again join

When the wings run out
I am left to scout
for the ones I can't bear to spare
pocketing them for different reasons
I like the ones depicting pretty seasons
long arms of trees reaching
Some in fall some in spring
I'll have to use them eventually

Once the shining quadruplets
are sitting in their snug slits
I push to hear their tumble in strife
as the washer rumbles to life

I'm left unsure if I can rest
without knowing if I've passed the quarter's test

*Withering Petals*

Roses are red, Violets are blue,
but I guess that's not entirely true.
Roses are me, Violets are she,
and sometimes I wish she was me.

Violet's charms define their bouquets,
neighboring flowers left in dismay.
Rose's gift giving implication,
asking to give to temptation,
unaware of her intimidation,
occasionally an apology after abrasions.

Violet's petals guide platonic beauty
Rose's thorns feign inherent cruelty.

Roses are accosted, Violets are exhausted.

Sharing in common the violent sorrow
the promise of being on display again tomorrow.

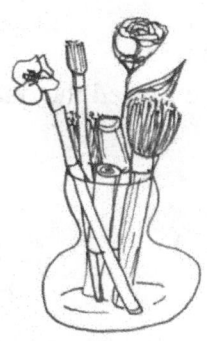

*Samson's Speed*

I can hardly believe
what my limbs can achieve
my shoes crunch curling leaves
while I lean into the breeze

It's my favorite time of year
to be running out here
where climbing uphill lacks fear
view of mountains so near

a tilt in my center of mass
shifting gears in an effort to pass
blurry stranger slipped by in a flash
taking care to avoid a crash

the long braid sweeping at my back
feels quite strange when I used to lack
the self control not to attack
any strand with a snip and snap

Samson believed it to be real
the strength he was able to steal
my quickening pace seals the deal
just to burn spite into appeal

pulling forest in my airway
feeling the trees blow my cares away
forever wishing I could stay
running under the trees
everyday

*Haunted*

Your family is a shadow
a group of ghosts I knew
it seems a soul ago
I grew with them and you

*Sisters*

Nightlights are lit
my sister and I sit
inquiring to the moon
when would be too soon
for our next adventure
ignorant to conjecture
we hum and whisper
stories of glorious spinsters
my only wish to the stars
is that these lives of ours
become tales of sin
we whisper over games of gin

*Before the Apple was Torn*

He's not me
and I'm not he
but I think I would be
an explosive sight to see
had I been born a he

Had I been born
before the apple was torn
perhaps my labor and scorn
would be seen as the norm

my screams and shouts
would not be pointless pouts
instead inciting righteous war
crowds chanting for more

*Where to Go*

My big brother leads the way
I'd follow him any day
He leads walking ahead
as I yap weaving threads
If ever we come to a fork in these dark woods
I know he'll choose better than I ever could
I'll walk just behind him
He'll ask if I can stop tripping him
I'll stick out my tongue in his direction
Throwing up a finger in silent inflection
Inside though, I hope he knows
Without him, I wouldn't know where to go

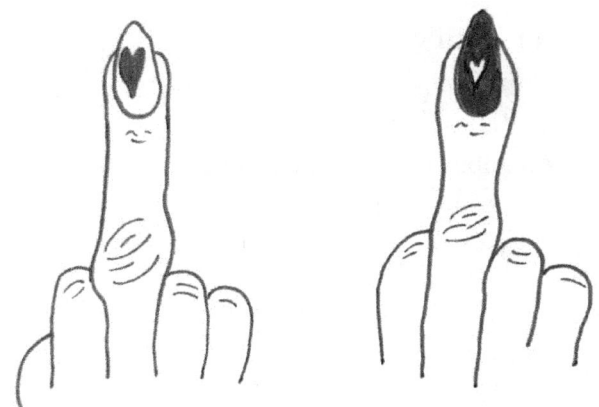

*Nylons*

at two years old
my skin was clear
with no experience to hold
but everything to hear

nylons slipped on my nana's legs
each and every day
the fabric catching as she begs
to keep the age at bay

sun marked and spotted calves
cracked and raised skin like braille
disappearing as she has
perfection in its trail

this is as essential to her
as slipping on shoes to leave the house
which to her goes by in a blur
but sticks in my brain like a louse

*Tired*

"The world is your oyster!"
Me? I've always found them a bit slimy
"There's hope on the horizon!"
but since the smog's got it grimy

My gaze has taken to the forest
Where my chest can expand
until the next fire season hits
bringing a tremor to my hands

Vision of leaves crisping to ash
my innocence crumbles with it
anyway, tonight I'll take out the trash
gripping to the tether of my spirit

next scrubbing at the never-ending dishes
staring through the glass pane over the sink
slowly counting on my hand the wishes
believing in them to keep me from the brink

my cracking heart confident I'll have my wishes come true
cherishing the proof in every stranger's smile
the proof that maybe every once in a while
I can believe in a sky that's bright blue

*Attempt to Cheer*

The lights are too bright
my skirt is too tight
the dotted crowd in the bleachers
unified beast of a creature

The band is off beat
laughter in the seats
the twelve of us stand together
huddled under stormy weather

The stands erupt
our boys are up
the end of the game is near
I used to love dancing here

The shift was slow
though I knew it showed
my lips attempt to form a smile
masking what's inside, what's vile

but all young girls can pretend
faking it until they make it in the end.

*Deck of Cards*

a comment on my beauty
will drill into my bones futiley
blowing down the grand deck of cards
of worries who try to consume me

I was just trying to dry my sweat
when you decided to place the bet
that I was stable enough to hear
your perception of all I fear

I don't trust mirrors and they don't trust me.

how are you supposed to know
the systemic kind of blow
a mere compliment from your lips
sends years of healing out the orbit

I'd rather stay hidden in layers
fears of losing lining my prayers
how my skin stretches over my bones
is mine to see, not yours to know

please avert your eyes and keep your lies.

*Past Selves*

My muscles grab along the actin and myosin
which is honestly quite kind of them
The trees of Forest Park become clearer
as my straining muscles pull me nearer

When at last I meet the shade
my troubles start to fade
Curling yellow leaves look brighter
even as my legs grow tighter

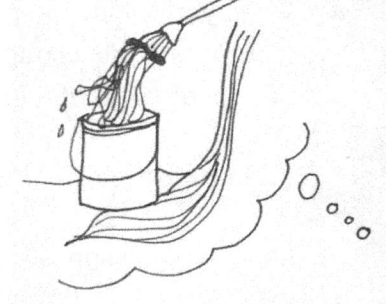

I pass a girl in all black attire
slowing my breath to admire
Her nonslick shoes
it'll give me the blues

Back to when I was the one in all black
the manager giving me flack in the back
For the no show coworker
as if I was some sort of conspirator

I nearly face plant over a root then
we all know what happens when
My focus shifts to the side
when it should be steadily on my stride.

*alone with me*

I prefer to be alone with me

It seems much easier to be
aware of the here and now
rather than wondering how
I must come across to you

You'll find it unlikely to be true
since I can't seem to shut up around you
That there's ever been a time
I've cared to mind

what others think
of little old me
to them I must be
the timidest version of me

You don't even flinch
as my hands hit my hips
"Did you just threaten me with a look?"
"Glad just one was all it took."

*forgotten spines*

I watched you take the sky
I watched you take the moon
I watched you claim the land
now you want the ocean too

You say there's aliens in there
new species you can cause despair
"We should go take a look!!" you pushed
I watched whistle-blowers be shushed

I watched the submarine implode
I watched how the new spaceship flew
I watched when it got stuck up there
and now they've missed the holidays too

planes are falling from the sky
companies distract you with treats
everyone wonders aloud why
as you step aboard and take your seat

You watch as forests burn
You watch species decline
You watch, you don't turn
Have you forgotten your
spines?

*Wrap It Up*

I care. I don't. I shouldn't.
I wouldn't-shouldn't, couldn't?
I'll say goodbye
Have one more cry
Mirroring the moon
Yearning mine to be soon
Is your train behind?
Are you biding your time?

# Winter

*Separate and Shared*

The sun has climbed her pedestal
the moon has gone to sleep
Their distance is quite technical
indifference slicing deep

*A rose is a rose is a rose*

A rose familiar with thorns
can recognize when to mourn
the moon cradles her then
a rose growing too thin
another spring will arrive
gifting a rose a new season to thrive
the moon can't help but smile
at the sight of her dissolving trials
until the darkness sneaks back in
the moon stretching to comfort her again

*Trepidation Station*

You are my favorite past time
you have the best relief
sometimes I'm left questioning
you want the best for me

You bring me to the summit
always left wondering if
someday I'll fall and plummet
off of this foggy cliff

It's a secret to admit
it's nice to sit up here
I just seem to find it fits
hope starts to feel quite near

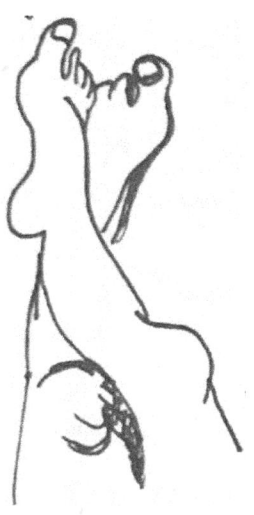

You whisper me sweet nothings
You scream at me in fright
I watch you and wonder if
You'll come for me at night.

*how to get back*

alcohol thins the veil of time
then and now blurring in my mind
one moment, I'm in my own body
the next I'm in hers
mine I guess,
from before yours
instead of his fingers on my knee
they're yours
and the only similarity
is how violently I want to rip them off of me
each blink goes from her to me
at once in my 24 year old body

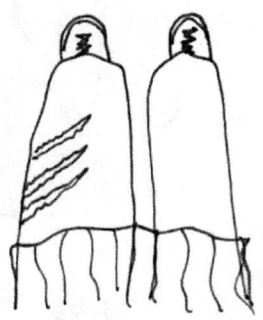

*Delicate Scarring*

Oh, to be a rose who grows
without the kind of thorn that shows
No delicate scarring
remnants of the marring
from where I cut you out

*Grateful and Hateful*

everything is small here
I really do try to hold it near
my temporary solitude
is fleeting gratitude

everything is boring here
everything is turning blue
it never once occurred to me
to hope for rescue

*the bin*

a long lost piece of me
seems it will always be
packed neatly in a bin
I can't bear to glance in

but you found a way to spark
the light in her that went dark
leaving me without a doubt
someday, I could let her out

perhaps you could really see
the bright light I used to be
without taking her from me
I wonder where I hid that key?

*Caught*

there's a shift in the air
when it's clear an agenda's near
collecting your receipts
so later your excuses can't be beat

I prefer not to play
though I'm often in dismay
to find there's no clean getaway
I'm trapped in this space to stay

stay playing your game of chess
no surprise you waited until my mind was a mess
alcohol tearing down the fortress
as you try to probe and assess

assess how to take my words and mold them
into a narrative tilted enough to tell him
without revealing just how grim
you behaved to achieve your whim

how women can look at one another
and decide it's her light that should be smothered
in order for her to be brighter to a man
who will never fully understand

*how to spot a foe*

I see you in the books I read
I hear you in the tales of woe
You're a lesson everyone should learn
in how to spot a foe

In the lines of history
going straight from A to B
it doesn't come so easily
with you standing in front of me

*Muffled*

That was my notebook all through college
my heart yearns for the knowledge
lost in all those days
I pushed writing away

It's not easy to face a calling
while ignoring the fear of falling
the phone's curt ringing sound
fades seamlessly into the background

Becoming white noise easy to ignore
right until I can't take it anymore
I have to pick up my pen again
calling to let the monsters in

I've spent days trying other ways
to keep the monsters at bay
running until my knees bled
but there was too much left unsaid

The phone rings away
day after day
while I scribble in ink
praying for a little relief

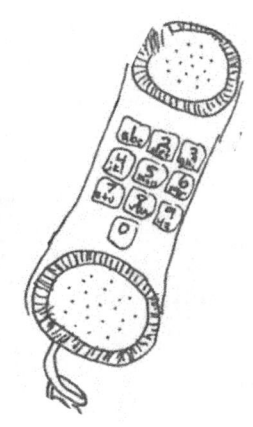

Searching for peace of mind
when I close the spine
Monsters now in neat lines
locked in this notebook of mine

So why can I still hear the ring of the line?

*the pitcher*

There is a dark space in the night
where I go back to our biggest fight

frosted pitcher sinking lower
your cup drains as mine gets fuller
your voice cuts deep, but your eyes cut deeper
no matter what I spit, mine look weaker

*Borrowed or Blue?*

If there's a piece of you in me, what's left of me in you?
Is it something borrowed or something blue?

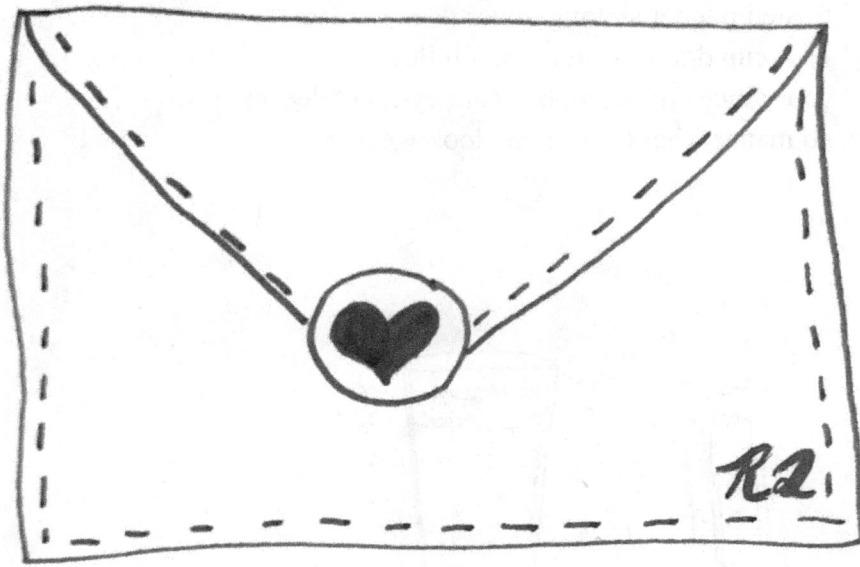

*the mirror*

a home with no mirrors
I can see myself clearer
I do everything
to avoid the sight of me

there used to be one in here
can you see me standing there?
shaking at the look
of everything they took

icey blue eyes
mountains for hips
there are no lies
see how my ribs dip?

see how my feet are stuck here?
but she's in the mirror there
four hands meet on glass
pushing to get past

can you see the cracks spread?
splitting through our heads
I bleed and try to be
one with her and me

my world crashes behind me
as I smash to my knees
fractions of her stare back
she's everything I lack

I just want her back.

*Recipe for Nostalgia*

I used to spend summers laughing with
my brother and the twins
I remember them now in the still
quiet of my kitchen
cutting frozen pizza but this time for one
I twirl the knife around slicing down
and suddenly they're just in the room next door
muffled laughs over Spongebob's world
One wants taquitos, one wants pizza,
but one will eat anything that little King
So I'll have a bit of each I think as my
attention subsides
and my brain is only filled with ideas of how to hide
the rotten piece of me on a bad day
to keep their innocent eyes away
but then a blink and it's just me in my apartment
closing up that twisted compartment
in me but it's too quiet
so I turn on my mixer the smell of
brownies playing trickster but the batter left
on the spatula, it's my brother's job to lick but
instead of being at my hip, he's at
home in bed by the light of his phone facing
the high school halls tomorrow on his own so I'll
turn on the sink to fill the bowl, staring as it
fills and fills my heart empties and empties
without my baby brother next to me

*Brief Grief*

first time seeing you in years
and my smile nearly reaches my ears
when you return my wary wave
as if to say it's ok

there's a trepidation in the air
which honestly, to be fair
deserves to take space here
even as my skin prickles in fear

the twist of my heart
when I realized with a start
all the things we left unsaid
in the quiet nods of our heads

going from best friend to acquaintance
is something I take to be adjacent
to losing a sister in a way
for it was grief we shared that day

*Currency*

Back to where we were
cars flying by in a blur
my attention so focused on the road ahead
my common sense slips on what shouldn't be said
Though stories always seem to be our common currency
I don't see the need for secrets between him and me
he's not quick to judge
and I'm not one to nudge
for details left unsaid
though I'll be the first to go ahead
with more than you want to know
part of me thinks his interest is just for show
to keep me awake and us alive
for the rest of this stormy drive

*Cliche*

it's quite a cliche
this display of my dismay
little miss "I can do it on my own"
having to face the reality of being all alone

at least I get to spread out in my bed
tossing & turning over words unsaid
remembering sidelong glances
I can stretch to long romances

I want the room to spin
with their slanted grin
a sweet forest breeze through the trees
is all he sees
when he thinks of me

# *Spring*

j'ai ete nomme pour une fleur qui
fleurit dans la printemp
qu'attendez vous plus de moi?
je ne voudrais jamais rien d'autre.

*Truth*

the sky is green
the grass is blue
I'm no longer
Mad at You

*Hunger*

I miss you in the mornings
I see you in the nights
I find it quite unnerving
I lost you in plain sight

You see me in the mornings
You miss me in the nights
You lost me without mourning
You find it quite alright

You came to be like sustenance
You found me quite a treat
I heard you as it was meant
I lost the urge to eat

I came to be alone with me
You were left with them
I love to sit here in the trees
My treat away from Him

*Pretty in Pink*

I wish there was a way
to thank her for that day
I noticed the pink clips in her hair
as her tight hug pushed away my air
Focusing on the bright blush on her cheeks
to ignore the mascara cascading down mine
Something has taken my ability to speak
but as she lets me go she seems to know
just what to do next as she brushes
me aside, lengthening her stride
announcing I'll be in a few to our professor
I would've kissed her for lesser

Then there was that day in the mailroom
concentrating to ignore the allure of her perfume
with the same destination it seemed
a natural inclination she offered me
a seat on her vespa, pink like those clips
my hands rest naturally on her hips
for the next few minutes of bliss
our packages rattle in the pink basket
I can pretend I got past it

*My cherry tree*

a cherry tree blossoms
on the hill I came to mourn
her soft pink petal on my thumb
wrinkles until she's torn

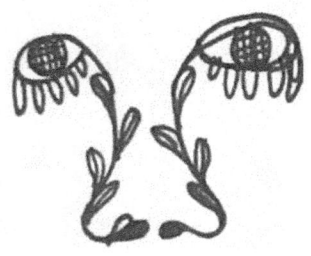

*is this a safe subject?*

I hate to make comparisons, so I won't.
I'll pretend I never said this, but you won't
stop being good to me, and you don't
even love me, and you don't
even have to. Do you remember

what you said that night? You stopped
to let me go ahead. You held
the door above my head. You said
it made sense. Did you see

the look on my face? How it felt as if
you tore me open to look in my chest? I hope
that never again, I'm left trailing behind like a pest.

*A Brain Like Me*

There's something to be said I guess
I read about the mental unrest
an innocent spring day can bring
for someone with a brain like me

It's unfair to be aware. to know
the chokehold of highs with
clairvoyance of impending lows
growing in my shrinking soul

Until the raisin inside
believes all the lies
my brain can concoct
I find beauty in rot

but that's in wintertime
and right now there's sunshine
green grass on which to lie
believing in longevity of blue skies

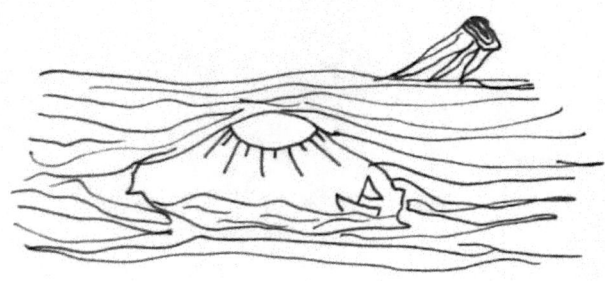

*Occupied*

I'm hearing tunes
In creaking rooms
Laughing at the shapes
Occupying empty space

Was that your voice?
Slicing past the noise?
Three of you here
None of you near
Each face swirls
I think I might hurl

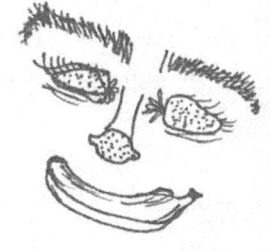

   one
        by
              one

You swirl into None

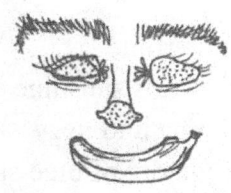

It was never real
But you see the appeal

*So It Goes*

Once curls cut short
in Winter he came back
he was quite fond
of all that I now lacked

By Spring he's gone
scissors back to their shelf
my locks are blond
I brush them now myself

*Perfection Perception*

I fear
He hears
My cares
Despite glares
His perception
of my reflection
Poises perfection

*All Me*

Yesterday, I'd say
me and you,
We're red and blue.
Today, I'd say
I'm purple, and you?
You haven't a clue
What could be your true hue.

*Purgatory*

It's Spring
I'm fun
I'm young
but not for long
You too
know it to be true
I see you hiding in the pew
He's not going to come
I imagine you'll feel quite glum
While I dance in the sun

*a warning*

I'm so lucky
I'm so sweet
I'm pretty enough to eat.
I won't show
You won't know
Until your breathing slows.
I may be lucky
I may be sweet
but Pretty can't be beat.

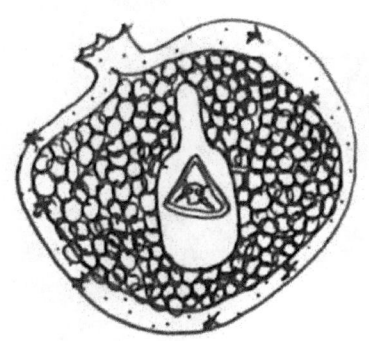

## In Wait

my sass will never leave me
swaying how to perceive me
she sits and waits
until someone needs a taste

*Jumping In*

The seat under me rumbles
as my focus crumbles
deep into the book in my lap
where it will stay caught in the trap
of finding something to read
quite like planting a seed
strangers come and go
I don't notice them though
roots growing in my minds eye
mighty wings of High Fae fly
the river in Boston glistens
as I take great care to listen
to writers who mirror themselves
in the books they place on their shelves
the squeal of brakes I don't hear
signal the end of my commute is near
I mark my spot with whatever I've got
standing to hop off at my stop
going on my merry way to start the day

*Who?*

I care to be,
You care to do.
I care to see,
You used to too.

There's always me,
There's always you.
How'd I get stuck between the two?

*Finally Me*

With this new comfort of ease in my bones
it's silly how much it pleases me to know it shows
On any given day in this new way
someone will stop to say
that I mirror my pretty name
or they like the energy I bring to a space
I finally understand the claim
with no one else to blame
but me growing into what
I was supposed to be
and shedding the old skin off of me
getting back to the beauty
that lies in my naivety.

*Scenery*

I miss you in the scenery, but that's no way for me to be.

# Acknowledgements

I want to first thank my Mom and Dad. The home and family you've built for us is my favorite part of my life. I love you both endlessly. Dad, your love of books and running gave me an incredible gift to get through the last 4 years, and the rest of my life. Mom, your openness, kindness, and nervousness are so beautiful, and I thank you for sharing them with me. To my siblings; Charlie, your dedication to our family as a big brother will always impress me. Thank you for setting the bar too high for me. Lucy, your art and loyalness are always my inspiration for continuing to write, thank you for never making fun of it. Tony, you've grown into the most amazing version of the boy I took care of. You've remained thoughtful and kind in a world that is not, and I love every minute I get to spend witnessing it. To my Nana and Papa, I know that you're reading these somehow, and the memories with you are still my happy place. To all my Cousins, Aunts, and Uncles, I think of you everyday. You've all saved me more than you know. I don't know how to thank my family enough.

To my girls, I love you with my whole heart. Thank you for always being there. Thank you for dancing with me through the hardest years. I can't wait to grow old with you.

To the writers I have spent thousands of hours crying with, thank you. I especially owe Rupi Kaur for the confidence I've gained and the inspiration for many of my first poems. I received her "Milk and Honey" poem collection for Christmas when I was 16. My mother gifted me the 10th edition of her collection this year, at 26 years old, and the memories of reading her words at 16 were overwhelming. Rupi Kaur, Louise Gluck, Emily Dickinson, Sylvia Plath, Virginia Wolff, and so many other women before me gave me the strength and inspiration for my words to grow with me in the last 20 years of my life.

I owe the vulnerability of accepting my "eccentricity" to Mark and Kurt Vonnegut. Mark's *Just Like Someone Without Mental Illness Only More So* reminded me of the fluidity of life and its phases. I am not always in bloom. John and Hank Green have shown me that writers come from their experiences. Many of my poems are deeply rooted in my education of science and anatomy, which Hank Green encapsulates so beautifully. John Green's many novels and essays have shaped my view of the world in so many ways, and I'm so thankful for his book *Looking for Alaska,* especially. Similarly, Brian Doyle's poetry has been with me through many nights when I was awoken from nightmares, and his words shape the safety of my sleep.

Finally: Thank *you* for reading. Thank you for sitting with me and seeing me. I hope you enjoyed it. I hope you give yourself the kindness you deserve to receive.

PS: I never thought I would be brave enough to put my poetry into the world. So I guess, thank you, little Rosie, for not giving up on your words. Your feelings are big, but they are so beautiful.

www.ingramcontent.com/pod-product-compliance
Lightning Source LLC
Chambersburg PA
CBHW060347050426
42449CB00011B/2854